CONTENTS

THE ORIGINS OF ROCKS

Our Earth is not a finished product. It is a system that is constantly shifting and changing. It has been on the move since it was created 4.5 billion years ago.

HOT STUFF

Earth began as a fiery ball of gases and dust that very slowly began to cool. As it cooled, the **crust** hardened into rock, and water droplets fell to create the oceans. This rock crust floats on a super hot layer of liquid rock called magma.

▲ *Planet Earth started as a ball of fire.*

COOLING OFF

Magma is made up of **elements** that can combine to form **minerals**. When magma cools and forms rock it is called crystallization. The different combinations of elements in the magma make different types of **igneous rock** when it cools. Slow cooling produces different rocks than fast cooling does.

▶ *Once magma reaches Earth's surface it is called lava.*

What Is the Rock Cycle?

Natalie Hyde

Crabtree Publishing Company

www.crabtreebooks.com

Author: Natalie Hyde
Editor-in-Chief: Paul Challen
Project coordinator: Kathy Middleton
Photo research: Melissa McClellan
Designer: Tibor Choleva
Proofreaders: Rachel Stuckey, Crystal Sikkens
Production coordinator: Amy Salter
Production: Kim Richardson
Prepress technician: Amy Salter

Consultant: Kelsey McCormack, BSc, MSc, PhD
McMaster University

Title page: Young boy climbing in Alps, Austria

Special Thanks: Stu Harding, Lucyna Bethune,
Sandor Monos and Sandee Ewasiuk

This book was produced for Crabtree Publishing
Company by Silver Dot Publishing.

Illustrations:
© David Brock: pages 7, 9

Photographs and reproductions:
© Dreamstime.com: title page (Tbroucek) and pages 5/6 large image (Juliengrondin), 10/11 large (Juliengrondin), 13 top (Kmowery3), 16/17 large (David Smith), 19 bottom (Erik De Graaf), 24 top (Vulkanette), 26 bottom (dmitriyd), 27/28 large (Aardlumens), 27 top (Indos82)
© istockphoto.com: headline image (susandaniels) and pages 5 bottom right (Karol Kozlowski),10 small image (koch valérie), 12 bottom photo (Zeichen und Sprache), 13 bottom (bponline), 20 small image (marekuliasz), 21 bottom left (raclro), 27 bottom (lissart), 29 middle (anniegreenwood)
© Shutterstock.com: background image: (schankz), and pages: 4 (Detelina Petkova), 5 middle (Matthew Jacques), 6/7 large (Kushch Dmitry), 8 (2009fotofriends), 10 large side image (Ronen),11 small photo (Alexander Gatsenko), 12 top photo (Jose Gil), 13/14 large (Alyona Burchette), 14 (Lance Bellers), 14 small image (sspopov), 16 small image (Clive Watkins), 17 top (syzx), 17 bottom (Jose Gil), 18 (Dorn1530), 19 top (gracious_tiger), 19 middle (Neale Cousland), 20/21 large (Anton Foltin), 21 middle (Holger Mette), 21 top (Yury Kosourov), 22 bottom (Zuleima), 22 top (Galyna Andrushko), 22 middle image (Ryan M. Bolton), 23 top (psamtik), 23 middle (Michael C. Gray), 23 bottom (robert paul van beets), 24/25 large (Roca), 25 top (Walter G Arce), 25 bottom left (Muellek Josef), 25 bottom right (Kenneth V. Pilon), 26 top (marekuliasz), pg 28 (Jeff R. Clow), 28 bottom (metalstock), 28/29 large (rtem), 29 bottom (DavidEwingPhotography)
© Prof saxx: page 19 upper middle
© AfriPics Images, photographersdirect.com: page 15 right
© NASA: page 5 bottom left

Library and Archives Canada Cataloguing in Publication

Hyde, Natalie, 1963-
   What is the rock cycle? / Natalie Hyde.

(Let's rock)
Includes index.
Issued also in an electronic format.
ISBN 978-0-7787-7231-6 (bound).--ISBN 978-0-7787-7236-1 (pbk.)

   1. Petrology--Juvenile literature. 2. Geochemical cycles--Juvenile literature. I. Title. II. Series: Let's rock (St. Catharines, Ont.)

QE432.2.H93 2011   j552   C2010-904134-8

Library of Congress Cataloging-in-Publication Data

Hyde, Natalie, 1963-
  What is the rock cycle? / Natalie Hyde.
    p. cm. -- (Let's rock)
  Includes index.
  ISBN 978-0-7787-7231-6 (reinforced lib. bdg. : alk. paper) -- ISBN 978-0-7787-7236-1 (pbk. : alk. paper) -- ISBN 978-1-4271-9525-8 (electronic (PDF)
  1. Petrology--Juvenile literature. 2. Geochemical cycles--Juvenile literature. I. Title. II. Series.

  QE432.2.H93 2011
  552--dc22
                                        2010024601

Crabtree Publishing Company

www.crabtreebooks.com   1-800-387-7650

Printed in the U.S.A./082010/BA20100709

Published in Canada
Crabtree Publishing
616 Welland Ave.
St. Catharines, Ontario
L2M 5V6

Published in the United States
Crabtree Publishing
PMB 59051
350 Fifth Avenue, 59th Floor
New York, New York 10118

Published in the United Kingdom
Crabtree Publishing
Maritime House
Basin Road North, Hove
BN41 1WR

Published in Australia
Crabtree Publishing
386 Mt. Alexander Rd.
Ascot Vale (Melbourne)
VIC 3032

MOONSCAPE

✳ The Tablelands in Gros Morne National Park in Newfoundland, Canada, look like the surface of the Moon. The flat-topped hills are made of peridotite, an igneous rock that is too toxic to support life. Formed in Earth's **mantle**, peridotite was pushed up to the surface when the Long Range Mountains in Newfoundland were formed.

▼ *Barren landscape caused by toxic rocks*

LIFE ON MARS?

✳ **Meteorites** are rocks that come from space. It is believed that the Allan Hills 84001 meteorite came from Mars. Scientists discovered something that looked like fossils of tiny bacteria in the rock. These fossils might be the first evidence of life on other planets.

RECIPE FOR MAKING MINERALS

Ingredients in Earth's crust:

oxygen	46.6%
silicon	27.7%
aluminum	8.1%
iron	5.0%
calcium	3.6%
sodium	2.8%
potassium	2.6%
magnesium	2.1%

Nature mixes different combinations of these elements to make all kinds of minerals. If oxygen and silicon mix, quartz is created. Magnesium and calcium carbonate will make dolomite. Oxygen and iron will make hematite.

▼ *This rock from Mars was found in Allan Hills, Antarctica in 1984.*

▼ *Hematite was used for making cylinder seals in Babylonia as early as 1900 BC.*

MOVING PLATES

Not too long ago scientists believed that the continents were fixed in place. We now know that the continents sit on **tectonic plates**, which are massive slabs of moving rock under Earth's surface. The continents create and destroy rock as they move.

THE BIG DRIFT

Millions of years ago, Earth's landmass was all in one piece surrounded by ocean. The moving magma underneath caused this supercontinent, called Pangaea, to break into smaller continents and begin drifting.

These pieces of crust began moving apart on one side and bumping into each other on the other. Where the tectonic plates spread apart, magma rose to the surface through the cracks. When this happened it formed volcanoes on land and ridges of new igneous rock in the ocean.

▶ *The supercontinent, Pangaea, was surrounded by ocean.*

THAT'S DEEP

✳ The Mariana Trench is the lowest point of Earth's crust. It has formed where the Pacific Plate is being pushed under the Mariana Plate in the Pacific Ocean. If you placed Mount Everest in the deepest spot, called Challenger Deep, there would still be 1.3 miles (2 km) of water above it!

RUMBLING EARTH

When the tectonic plates slide past each other, they stick and grind. This movement causes tremors and earthquakes. One plate is sometimes pushed under the other. This part of the Earth's crust sinks into the mantle where the heat melts the rocks back into magma.

CRUSTY STUFF

When two tectonic plates **collide** the crust is folded, buckled, and thrust upward, causing mountains to form. The heat and pressure can cause changes to igneous and **sedimentary rocks**, turning them into **metamorphic rocks**.

COLLIDING PLATES

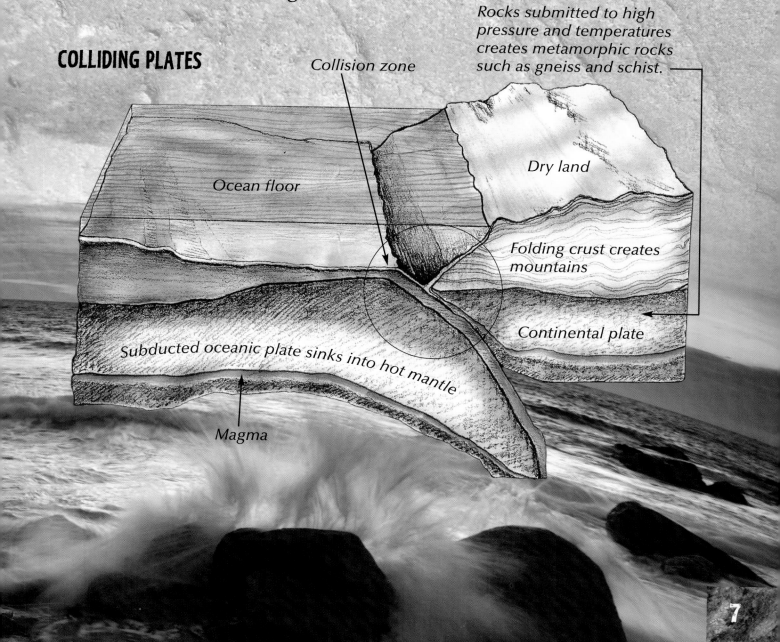

Rocks submitted to high pressure and temperatures creates metamorphic rocks such as gneiss and schist.

Collision zone

Ocean floor

Dry land

Folding crust creates mountains

Subducted oceanic plate sinks into hot mantle

Continental plate

Magma

THE ROCK CYCLE

Earth is a system that is constantly **recycling** and reusing materials. This is especially true of the rock cycle.

STARTING OUT

All rocks begin as molten magma deep inside Earth. Eventually the magma cools and turns into a solid. This can happen under or above ground but both types are called igneous rocks.

WEARING AWAY

Once igneous rocks are brought to the surface, forces in nature begin to wear away at the rock. This process, called weathering, happens slowly over time. Wind, water, chemicals, and ice all help to break down rock into small particles called sediment.

SHORTCUTS!

✳ The rock cycle is not always a perfect circle. At times igneous rock does not reach the surface, remaining deep underground. If exposed to **intense** heat and pressure it can turn into metamorphic rock.

Igneous rocks are not the only rocks that create the sediment that forms sedimentary rock. Metamorphic and sedimentary rocks also undergo weathering.

▼ *In time, even these sharp peaks of the Castle Mountain in Banff National Park, Alberta, Canada, will be worn down by weathering.*

EROSION IN MOTION

The same forces that cause the rocks to weather also move the sediment. This is called erosion. Particles are carried by wind, rivers, or glaciers downward until they collect in layers. Over time the layers of sediment build up and are **cemented** together to form sedimentary rock.

IT'S GETTING HOT!

As the plates shift, sedimentary rock is **exposed** to new forces. Intense heat and pressure from mountain building or magma change the rock's structure. It will form metamorphic rock.

MELTING MAGMA

Metamorphic rock that is pushed deeper into the mantle of Earth heats up until it melts, turning back into magma.

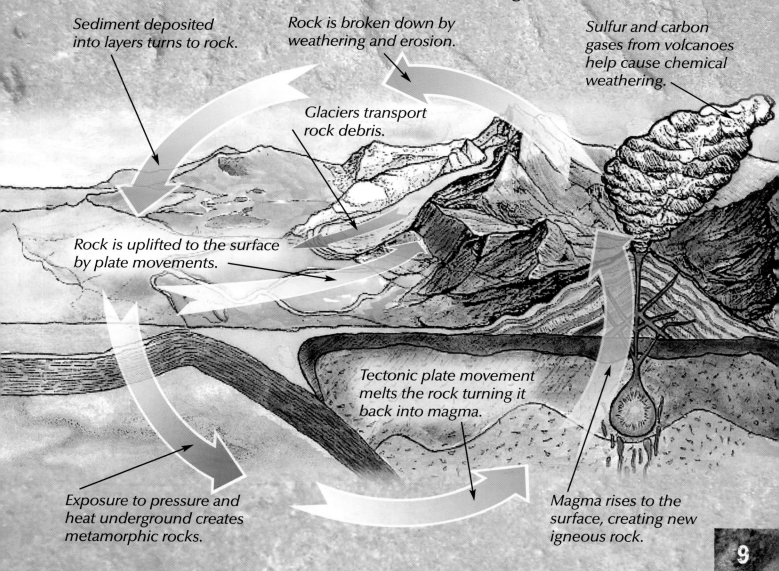

Sediment deposited into layers turns to rock.

Rock is broken down by weathering and erosion.

Sulfur and carbon gases from volcanoes help cause chemical weathering.

Glaciers transport rock debris.

Rock is uplifted to the surface by plate movements.

Tectonic plate movement melts the rock turning it back into magma.

Exposure to pressure and heat underground creates metamorphic rocks.

Magma rises to the surface, creating new igneous rock.

EXPLOSIVE STUFF!

The rock cycle often begins with volcanoes. These fiery mountains are places where magma has reached the surface and new rock is created.

▼ Mount Bromo is an active volcano in East Java, Indonesia.

PIPES AND VENTS

Volcanoes are found near cracks in Earth's crust. Magma pushes up through these weak spots and creates a round **channel** called a pipe. The pipe ends at the surface at an opening called a vent.

As the magma begins to spill out and cool, pieces of rock and ash build up around the vent, creating a cone-shaped mountain.

▶ Flowing lava can destroy everything in its path.

HEAVY METALS

Magma that contains a lot of iron and **magnesium** flows easily. It oozes onto the surface through cracks in the crust.

GETTING STUCK

Silicon and aluminum are elements that are "sticky." They don't flow easily. This type of magma usually builds up under pressure and is then released very quickly. The explosion is very violent and dangerous.

▼ *Active volcanoes often spew clouds of volcanic ash.*

MAKE A VOLCANO

(This activity needs adult supervision.)

You will need:

- ½ cup water
- ¼ cup dishwashing liquid
- ¼ cup vinegar
- 2 or 3 drops of red and yellow food coloring
- clean bottle or pitcher
- ¼ cup baking soda
- small can or jar
- sand or dirt

Mix the water, dishwashing liquid, vinegar, and food coloring in the bottle or pitcher. Put the baking soda into the can or jar. Outside, bury the can or jar in a pile of sand or dirt, leaving the lip of the can or jar sticking out. Pour a little of the mixture from the pitcher into the can and watch it bubble up and over—just like lava from a volcano.

The gas created by the baking soda and vinegar makes the liquid bubble up, just like the underground gas that causes the magma to rise and erupt.

◄ *Red-hot magma spills out of the opening of a volcano called a vent.*

HEATING AND COOLING

Igneous rocks can form above or below ground. Magma that rises through cracks in the crust cools very quickly when it meets air. When magma cannot find a path to the surface through a volcano, it sometimes cools deep below ground. This creates a very different type of igneous rock.

TRAPPED

Intrusive igneous rocks form deep underground. Magma that is trapped in a huge magma chamber cools very slowly. These rocks have large grains and are much **denser** and harder than those formed on the surface.

STICKING OUT

Extrusive igneous rocks form outside Earth's crust. Their grains are very fine and scientists often need a microscope to see which minerals are present.

▶ *These columns are made of an extrusive igneous rock called basalt.*

▲ *Cooled lava creates barren landscapes called lava fields.*

TAKING A "BATH"

When the magma in a huge magma chamber crystallizes, it creates a massive rock. This massive rock structure is known as a batholith. Most batholiths extend over thousands of square miles, forming large mountain ranges.

▼ *The granite crest of Half Dome in Yosemite National Park, California, rises more than 4,737 feet (1,444 m) above the valley floor.*

STRANGE STRUCTURES

Mountain building and erosion bring intrusive rocks to the surface. They create very interesting rock structures. Magma that cools in **vertical** cracks creates tall, narrow ridges of hard rock called dikes. Magma that flows sideways through sedimentary rock forms a flat hard rock layer called a sill.

▼ *Devils Backbone in Crater Lake National Park, Oregon, is a dike.*

GOING UP!

❋ Yosemite National Park in California is known for its granite cliffs and waterfalls. They are the remains of huge granite batholiths. El Capitan is the park's 3000-foot (914 m) high granite cliff that was formed 103 million years ago.

▶ *El Capitan is one of the world's most popular challenges for rock climbers.*

IGNEOUS ROCK TYPES

Igneous rocks come in many different sizes and colors. The rocks are made up of different crystals, depending on which elements are in the magma and where and how fast the magma cools.

STEPPING ALONG

Basalt is an extrusive igneous rock with very fine grains that forms when lava flows cool. The magma from underwater volcanoes cools so quickly that the basalt rocks are pillow-shaped. On land lava may shrink when it cools. This causes the rock to form **fractures**, cracking the basalt into six-sided columns that look like stepping stones.

BUILDING BLOCKS

Granite is formed when magma cools slowly deep inside Earth. It has large crystals that make it a tough, hard rock that is useful for construction.

▶ The Giant's Causeway in Northern Ireland is the result of an ancient volcanic eruption. About 40,000 basalt columns were created.

▼ Granite comes in a range of colors, from pink to gray or sometimes black.

HOT OR NOT?

(This activity needs adult supervision.)

This experiment will show how magma cools quickly and slowly produces different igneous rocks.

You will need:

- small cooking pot
- 2 cups of water
- Epsom salts
- 2 clean jars
- 2 pipe cleaners

Heat the water in the cooking pot until it is near boiling. Stir Epsom salts into the liquid until no more will dissolve. Divide the mixture into two separate jars. Take two pipe cleaners and wrap them into coils. You can wrap them around a pencil and then carefully remove them. Put one pipe cleaner in each jar. Place one jar in the refrigerator and leave the other one at room temperature. Leave the experiment for at least 24 hours. Compare the results.

How does temperature affect crystal formation?

GOING UNDERGROUND

Kimberlite is a **subvolcanic** rock that forms in the underground pipes of volcanoes. It has medium-sized grains and often also contains gemstones such as diamonds and garnets.

▼ *This mine engineer examines a Kimberlite rockface in the Cullinan Diamond mine in South Africa.*

EROSION IN ACTION

Once rocks have begun to break down through weathering, erosion takes over. Erosion and gravity move the particles to places where they begin the process of making sedimentary rock.

WIND DELIVERY

Wind erosion can move particles over large distances. The smaller the particles, the farther they can travel. When the wind speed slows, the sediment is dropped.

▼ Tower-like stone formations created by wind erosion

DIGGING UP THE PAST

✳ Dinosaur Valley is the section of the Red Deer River Valley near Drumheller, Alberta, Canada. Wind and water erosion has exposed hundreds of dinosaur skeletons in the 70-million-year-old rock.

▼ Albertosaurus lived more than 70 million years ago. Its habitat was restricted in range to the modern-day Canadian province of Alberta.

WATER POWER

Water is one of the most powerful forces of erosion. Over time, rivers and streams can wear down even hard metamorphic rock. Moving water transports tons of sediment every day. Larger pieces slide along riverbeds and ocean floors in strong currents. Smaller particles are **suspended** in the water and deposited where the river bends or slows.

▲ *The eroded material carried away by rivers is called the load.*

THE ROOT CAUSE

Even plants help erode rock. Their roots grow into small cracks in rocks to help anchor the plant. As the roots grow, the cracks widen, eventually splitting the rock.

▼ *Roots of plants can split even huge rocks.*

ICE IS NICE

Glaciers are large ice masses that move slowly down mountains. Because the ice is heavy and sharp, rocks are broken down and pushed along as the glacier carves out new valleys. Once the glaciers melt, the rock fragments and sediment are **deposited**.

LAYERED ROCK

Wind, water, and ice all help to move eroded material from rocks to new locations. These layers are the beginning of new sedimentary rock.

SEDIMENTARY STATUS

Sedimentary rock forms wherever layers of sediment and rock fragments build up. Over time these **strata** are pressed and cemented together.

VARIATIONS

Different types of sediment make different types of sedimentary rocks. Rock formed with sediment that comes from weathered rocks is called clastic rock. All types of rock—igneous, sedimentary, and metamorphic— can form new sedimentary rock.

CRYSTALLIZING CHEMICALS

Chemicals can form inorganic sedimentary rock. Salt, silica, and calcite that are **dissolved** in water can crystallize when the water **evaporates**.

HISTORY LESSON

✱ By studying the make-up of different layers in sedimentary rock, scientists can "read" the environment of the area over time. Layers of seashell particles tell researchers that the area was once under water. A layer of ash points to a nearby volcanic eruption. Sandstone might show a time of **drought** or desert conditions.

▼ Tufa rocks in Mono Lake, California, are formed from deposits of calcite.

DRIP... DRIP... DRIP...

Water dripping through cracks in the ceilings of caves often contains minerals. As the water evaporates, the minerals are left behind, which produces rock icicles called stalactites. When the water drips to the floor of a cave, mineral towers called stalagmites form. Hard mineral columns are created where stalactites and stalagmites meet.

▲ During the **Stone Age**, people painted astonishing pictures on rock walls deep inside caves. Most cave paintings focused on hunters and animals.

▲ Minerals in caves can help create very interesting formations.

▼ Coal was formed from plants like cycads that still grow today.

GOING ORGANIC

Material that comes from living things is organic. Some organic materials also form sedimentary rocks. Leaves, stems, and bark that **decay** very slowly in swamps can form layers of sediment. As these layers are buried deeper underground, heat and pressure cause this material to form an organic sedimentary rock such as coal.

SEDIMENTARY ROCK TYPES

The different types of material that make sediment create rocks with very different shapes, colors, and **textures**.

FLAKEY STUFF

Shale is a type of sedimentary rock made from clay or mud and other minerals. It forms at the bottom of deep water environments or slow-moving streams. Shale flakes easily between its layers and this is where scientists find many fossils and animal tracks.

SAND IS GRAND

Sand is made up of tiny pieces of other rocks. That is why some beaches around the world are pure white, while others are tan, red, or black. Sandstone is made from layers of sand that have been **compressed** and cemented together. Like sand, sandstone comes in a variety of colors. Sometimes the different sand layers create a striped sandstone.

▶ Antelope Canyon is one of the most breathtaking places on Earth. It was carved from the colorful Navajo sandstone over thousands of years.

▼ Sand samples showing the variety of colors

FIRE!

✳ Flint is a special sedimentary rock often found in chalk and limestone. It was used in the Stone Age to create tools and start fire. If struck with steel or iron pyrite, flint makes a spark. This was the early humans' fire starter!

▼ *The control of fire by early humans was a turning point in our evolution.*

MIX IT UP!

You will need:
- sand, pebbles, and small rocks of different sizes and colors
- plaster of Paris
- large bowl
- water

Mix the plaster of Paris and water in the bowl, according to the package directions. Mix in sand, pebbles, and rocks. Form the mixture into a ball and let dry.

You have created your own conglomerate rock!

▼ *A large boulder of conglomerate rock*

COMING TOGETHER

Large pieces of rocks can be cemented together to make conglomerates. In many of these rocks, large pieces of stones made smooth by flowing water can easily be seen. Breccia, a type of conglomerate, also has large pieces of rock, but they have sharp edges.

FANTASTIC FOSSILS

Fossils are traces of organisms preserved in rock. Sedimentary rock is the only stage in the rock cycle where fossils are found.

TOO MUCH PRESSURE

The magma that cools to make igneous rocks is so hot that it completely destroys any material it touches. Metamorphic rock undergoes intense heat and pressure. This ruins any fossils that may have been in the original rock.

TRAPPED!

Fossils are created when organic material such as leaves, insects, or shells becomes trapped in sediment. The layers of sediment keep the material from decaying. As the layers harden, an impression is left in the rock.

A STICKY SITUATION

✳ Some insects and even small tree frogs can become trapped in sticky tree resin. The resin preserves the bodies and eventually hardens into amber.

▼ *Frog preserved in Baltic amber*

▼ *Prehistoric shells fossilized in layers of sedimentary rock*

BIG BONES

Entire dinosaur skeletons have been found in sedimentary rock. Some are over 120 feet (37 m) long! One dinosaur has recently been discovered in North Dakota that is partly mummified. Parts of its tissue and skin are visible.

▲ Reconstructed dinosaur skeletons can be seen in museums all around the world.

▼ *Paleontologists must be careful not to damage hidden parts of fossils.*

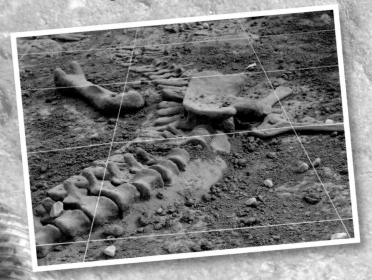

SURFACING

Fossils are brought to the surface by mountain building and erosion. Paleontologists use fossils to study **prehistoric** life. They are one of the most important records of that time. By studying fossilized plants and animals, scientists can learn about life millions of years ago.

STONE TREES

Wood that is buried under sediment can change to rock. The organic material is replaced with minerals and is called petrified wood. Areas where many trees have been preserved this way are called petrified forests.

▼ *Petrified wood (from the Greek root "petro" meaning "rock") literally means "wood turned into stone."*

METAMORPHIC ROCKS

Heat and pressure cause a rock to change its structure, texture, and color. Rocks that have undergone these changes are called metamorphic rock.

MAKING CONTACT

Magma that pushes its way to the surface through cracks in Earth's crust creates magma chambers and pipes, which create volcanoes. As the magma moves upward, the heat changes the rock it touches, but doesn't melt it. This is called contact metamorphism.

▲ *The intense heat of magma can change surrounding rocks.*

THE REGIONAL SCENE

When Earth's tectonic plates collide, the rock can buckle and fold creating mountains. The farther down rock is pushed, the more heat and pressure is applied. Mountain building is the main source of metamorphic rocks. Because it happens over a large area, it is called regional metamorphism.

▶ *The Alps were created by regional metamorphism.*

UNDER PRESSURE

You will need:

- different colors of play dough or modeling clay

Make three balls from clay of different colors to represent rock particles. Roll them together into one ball. Smash it flat like a fat pancake. Stand it on its edge and smash it flat again. Cut it into fours. Look at the cut edges to see how the pressure has made the colors stick together. This is how the minerals in metamorphic rocks stick together after being subjected to the heat and pressure deep inside Earth.

BIG IMPACT

The shock waves created when material crashes into Earth or during underground explosions can also cause changes to the crystals in rock. Rocks changed by shock metamorphism have been found in **meteorite** craters and at nuclear test sites.

▲ Meteorite craters often contain rocks changed by the pressure from the forces of impact.

▼ Green moldavites are tektites found in Europe.

▼ Indochinite, a tektite from Thailand, is believed to be 700,000 years old.

SHOCKING!

✳ Tektites are natural glass rocks formed when meteorites crash into Earth. They are usually black or olive green and found in the area around impact craters.

METAMORPHIC ROCK TYPES

This stage of the rock cycle can create many different types of rock. The structure and texture of the new rock depends on the amount of heat and pressure and also the type of **parent rock.**

GREAT SLATE

Low heat and pressure can turn igneous rocks such as mudstone and shale into slate. Slate breaks easily into flat sheets and is often used as roof tiles.

▲ *Slate is a low-grade contact metamorphic rock.*

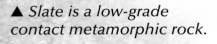
▶ *535-million-year-old gneiss formations in Chimney Rock State Park, North Carolina*

ALL THE MARBLES

Sedimentary limestone that undergoes heat and pressure during mountain building can change into marble. Marble is not a very hard stone and is prized for use in buildings and **sculptures.** It is often white but particles in the limestone can cause it to be pink, gray, green, and even black.

▶ *Red marble has been valued for its natural beauty since the dawn of civilization.*

▲ *Anthracite has the highest carbon count of all coals.*

VERY "GNEISS"!

Extremely high heat and pressure can turn the igneous rock granite into gneiss (pronounced "nice"). Gneiss is a foliated metamorphic rock. As the rock formed, the crystals rearranged themselves into bands or stripes. Other metamorphic rocks, such as quartzite, do not have a striped pattern and are nonfoliated.

WARMING UP

Coal is an organic sedimentary rock that is an important source of fuel. Coal that is pushed deep inside Earth can turn into anthracite. This metamorphic rock burns hotter without creating soot, which made it a popular heat source.

GEMS AND JEWELS

❋ Gemstones are colorful minerals that are used in jewelry and decorations. They are sometimes formed under the same heat and pressure that forms metamorphic rock. Schist and gneiss often contain rubies, sapphires, garnet, and jade.

▲ *Garnet crystals are often found in gneiss rock.*

PEOPLE AND ROCKS

Each step in the rock cycle provides **humanity** with important materials for daily life.

IN YOUR HOUSE

We can find igneous rocks right in our own homes. Granite is sometimes used for kitchen countertops because it is so hard. Lava rocks, such as pumice stones, help keep our skin smooth.

BUILDING STONE

Sedimentary rocks are used as building stones because they are easy to find and can be cut easily into blocks. Bridges, churches, government buildings, and monuments have all been made of this useful rock. Even the sediment that is the beginning of sedimentary rocks is useful. Sand and gravel are mined to make cement and concrete.

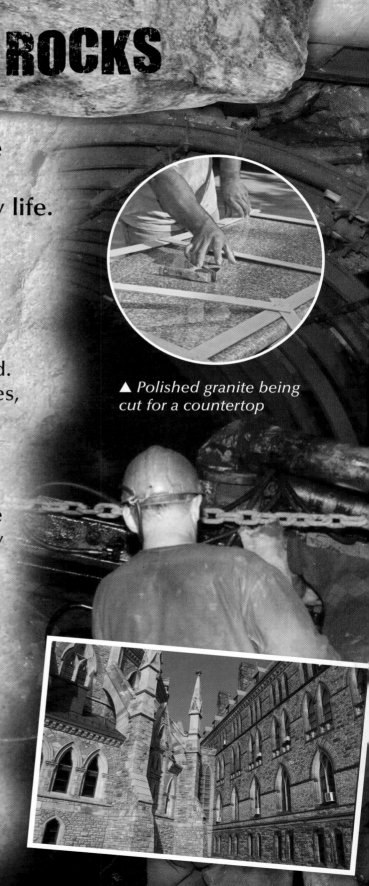

▲ *Polished granite being cut for a countertop*

▶ *Much of the exterior of Parliament Hill in Ottawa, the capital of Canada, was built using Nepean sandstone, quarried nearby.*

PARIS UNDERGROUND

✳ Most buildings and bridges in Paris, France, are made of limestone. The quarry is not hard to find...it is under the city. Hundreds of miles of tunnels under Paris are the remains of limestone quarries. Now the tunnels are the Catacombs—tombs containing the bones of dead citizens.

▼ *The Catacombs house the remains of approximately six million Parisians.*

CARVING IT OUT

Marble is a metamorphic rock with many uses. Incredible sculptures, such as Michelangelo's *David*, are made from marble. The Taj Mahal in Agra, India, is a breathtaking marble **mausoleum** made of pure white marble.

◀ *Coal is often mined in underground mines.*

LOOKING BACK

The fossils found in sedimentary rocks are our only record of prehistoric life on Earth. Without these traces of plants and animals, we would have very little knowledge of what Earth was like thousands of years ago.

FIRED UP!

Coal has been a vital source of fuel for hundreds of years. Even now, coal-fired power plants provide electricity to millions of people.

▼ *The sculpture of David was moved to Accademia Gallery in Florence, where it attracts many visitors.*

GLOSSARY

cemented Particles glued together with minerals

channel Passageway in Earth's crust

collide Crash together

compressed Pressed tightly together

continents A large landmass on Earth

crust The outer part of Earth

decay Slow rotting of dead plants and animals

denser The particles are crowded closer together

deposited Dropped or set down

dissolved In a solution

drought A long time with no rainfall

elements Substances that cannot be separated into simpler substances

evaporates Loses liquid into the air

exposed Open to the weather

fractures Breaks or cracks

humanity All living humans on Earth

igneous rock Formed by the cooling of magma or lava

intense Very strong

magnesium A silver-white metallic element

mantle The layer of Earth between the crust and the core

mausoleum A large burial chamber, usually above ground

metamorphic rock Formed from an existing rock that has been changed due to heat and pressure

meteorites Rocks from space that fall to Earth

minerals Solids formed from elements in nature

parent rock The original rock that another type of rock was formed from

prehistoric Belonging to a time before recorded history

preserved Kept from decaying or spoiling

recycling Reusing materials for new products

sculptures Artwork made by shaping stone or wood

sedimentary rock Formed from layers of deposited sediment

Stone Age A prehistoric period when tools were made from stone

strata Layers of rock

subvolcanic Existing below a volcano

suspended Kept from falling

tectonic plates Massive slabs of moving rock beneath the ground

textures The feel of surfaces

vertical Something that is straight up and down

MORE INFORMATION

FURTHER READING

Rocks, Minerals, and Resources series.
   Crabtree Publishing, 2004/2005.

Metamorphic Rocks And The Rock Cycle.
   Mattern, J.; Powerkids Press, 2006.

Rocks and Minerals.
   Britannica Illustrated Science Library, 2009.

The Rock Cycle.
   Ostopowich, M.; Weigl Publishers Inc., 2005.

WEBSITES

Mineralogy 4 Kids
www.minsocam.org/MSA/K12/rkcycle/rkcycleindex.html

Rocks for Kids
www.rocksforkids.com/RFK/howrocks.html

Rocks and Minerals
http://42explore.com/rocks.htm

Kids' Crossing
http://eo.ucar.edu/kids/green/cycles8.htm

The Rock Key
www.rockhounds.com/rockshop/rockkey/index.html

Geology for Kids
www.kidsgeo.com/geology-for-kids/

INDEX